I Know Sousa, Not

A Survival Guide for the Band Director Teaching Choirs

Russell L. Robinson

HERITAGE MUSIC PRESS

a Lorenz company • www.lorenz.com

Editors: Kris Kropff and Mary Lynn Lightfoot
Book Design: Digital Dynamite, Inc.
Cover Design: Jeff Richards

Heritage Music Press
A division of The Lorenz Corporation
P.O. Box 802
Dayton, OH 45401-0802
www.lorenz.com

Printed in the United States of America

ISBN: 978-1-4291-0356-5

To all of the instrumentalists who, like me, have entered the world of choral music. May the added beauty of voices and text enrich your musical life.

CONTENTS

FOREWORD

Hello. My name is Russell Robinson and I'm a former band director. There, I said it! I was trained at the undergraduate level as a band director and thought I would be a band director forever. My first teaching position was in Cassville, Missouri. I was to be the Assistant Band Director to John Knight, at that time one of the finest band directors in the state of Missouri. (Dr. Knight went on to a highly successful career as a Professor of Music Education and Wind Symphony conductor at Oberlin Conservatory.) He had garnered many years of straight superior ratings at district and state evaluation festivals (or, as we used to call them, contests).

Upon my arrival, I discovered that along with the duties of Assistant Band Director, my schedule included teaching choirs! I had grown up singing in church, attended a summer music camp in high school where we instrumentalists *could* sing in the choir, and sang in the college choir my senior year, but that was the extent of my choral training. My teaching schedule in Cassville included three middle school general music classes, middle school jazz band, sixth-grade band, and high school choir. My first high school choir had 17 members: 11 girls and six guys, five of whom thought they were basses. I identified a few of those "basses" as tenors. Then, I quickly turned my general music classes into part-time choirs. We sang two days a week, did general music activities two days a week, and had music listening one day a week.

As a trained band director, I had no real idea what I was doing. I had little choral training. I knew nothing about warm-ups, vowels, or breathing (or I didn't think I did). And when it came to literature...a piece that my college choir performed in my senior year was the John Ness Beck *Canticle of Praise*. So, of course, my high school choir was going to sing that too! Let's see: my college choir of 70 singers did it, so why not my 17-member high school choir? I was going to do it if it killed them. And, it almost did!

I kept working at teaching this "new" ensemble, the choir. I returned to the university and took classes to earn my lifetime certification in choral music, K–12 (scary, but back then it was a lifetime certification). What I soon realized was that, given some basic fundamentals, I could quickly create a credible choir and acceptable music out of just about anyone who ended up in the ensemble, whereas with the band, it took a lot of time, maintenance of instruments, manual dexterity, etc. to produce an ensemble and quality music. This is when I fell in love with choral music and out of love with marching band. We had to march a different show on the field every Friday night back then, and believe me, I developed the greatest respect for good marching band directors. Then, there was the addition of text! We didn't have text in band music. How much easier it was to know where to place the rise and fall of the music, the tensions and releases, the accents, etc., because with choir we have text!

By the time I left Cassville six years later, we had over 140 in the choral program in a school with 450 students. My program included the cheerleaders and football players (who still go hand in hand) and they became a legitimate choir. I also had a show choir (we called them swing choirs back then). Just as our jazz band members had to be in the concert band, the concert choir was a requirement for all swing choir members.

Now, over 30 years later, this "old" band director has been in choral music ever since, from public school and university teaching, to writing and arranging, to being a clinician and conducting all over the world. I love choral music! And I love helping other people teach it better if I can. These two loves first coalesced into a clinic, as I became aware of just how many band and orchestra directors were teaching choral music in some way. I estimate that 60 percent of trained instrumental music education majors find themselves either teaching choral music in schools or directing church choirs. Often, these band-turned-choral directors will not attend a choral or vocal clinic at a convention for fear that a "basic" question about vowels, warm-ups, literature, etc., will lead to embarrassment. They will, however, attend a clinic specifically for them, as teachers in similar situations will populate the room.

This book grew out of those clinics, and many of the ideas, techniques and anecdotes included here have been generated from teachers in my clinics or from interactions through my university teaching role. It is my hope that it will help you succeed in your new role and ultimately discover the many joys that can come from directing choirs.

ACKNOWLEDGEMENTS

I would like to thank Mary Lynn Lightfoot, Choral Editor at Heritage Music Press, for giving me the idea to write this book after attending one of my workshops. I would also like to thank Kris Kropff, Literary Editor for The Lorenz Corporation, for helping make sense of my stream-of-consciousness writing. As a former band director, I have been doing workshops on this topic at conventions for many years. Writing this has allowed me to organize my thoughts, and I'm sure that my workshops will be improved as a result of writing this.

I would also like to thank my wife, Brenda, who assisted me in the ideas, writing and editing of the initial manuscript. I appreciate her assistance and patience more than words can express.

Finally, I thank all of the many music teachers who I have observed, worked with, and who have attended my workshops for allowing me to learn so much from them in our interactions. I hope that the ideas and techniques in this book are helpful to all of those hard working music teachers (former and current instrumental teachers included) who are teaching choirs on a regular basis.

STRANGER IN A NOT-SO-STRANGE LAND

A LOOK INSIDE THE CHORAL CLASSROOM AND AT THE MANY SKILLS BAND DIRECTORS ALREADY BRING TO IT

While there appear to be differences in the teaching techniques of both disciplines—and okay, let's be honest, there are actual differences—the good news is that those trained as instrumental conductors are actually in a much better position to direct a choir than the average choir director is to direct a band. At the risk of upsetting my choral colleagues, I would even go so far as to suggest that many choir directors could learn a thing or two from band directors.

THE EXTRA-MUSICAL MATTERS

Instrumental directors generally and by necessity have excellent organizational skills. Why? Band and orchestra directors have to deal with a lot of "stuff"—spit valves, reeds, ligatures, corks, march-

Instrumental conductors are actually in a much better position to direct a choir than the average choir director is to direct a band.

ing flip folders, tuners, music stands, rosin, bows, school-owned instruments, band uniforms. You can't continually buy that which you do not maintain (e.g., scores, band uniforms, double basses, tubas); without organization, band directors simply cannot survive. These organizational skills will serve you well in teaching choral music.

MANAGING THE CHORAL MUSIC LIBRARY

If one walks into a band or orchestra library, one will usually find the music easily accessible. Choral libraries tend to be at the other end of the organizational spectrum.

If one walks into a band or orchestra library, one will usually find the music easily accessible. When one delves further, he or she will more often than not find the music within the library in order; all of the parts will be there and generally in good "working order" regardless of the year the score and parts were purchased. Choral libraries tend to be at the other end of the organizational spectrum.

In one of my choral workshops, I ask choral directors a series of questions ranging from how they manage mainstreaming, curriculum, the first week of school, etc. It is a great opportunity for veteran choral teachers to share their experiences and ideas with younger teachers and vice versa. One of the questions I ask is, "How do you organize your choral library?" Somewhat like the person in church who hears something from the minister that "hits home," I will see guilt-stricken looks come over the directors' faces. I then ask, "*Do* you organize your library? If I walked into your choral library right now, would I find everything organized, by title, the music still as nice as when you first purchased it?" At that point, in a crowd of 100 or so, there will be only a few who don't look at least a little uncomfortable. I joke that a colleague of mine has every piece of music she has ever done with her choir in the past 30 years *somewhere* in her office!

Music is too expensive to use it just once. Organize your choral library the way you would (or did, or maybe even still do) your band or orchestra library, with music easily accessible, in order, complete, and generally in good "working order," regardless of the year it was purchased. And just as you wouldn't photocopy a band score and parts, never photocopy your choral music, no matter how tempting it may be! It is illegal, thereby sending a very poor message to your students, who know it is illegal. Your principal knows too.

Organize your choral library the way you would your band or orchestra library.

REHEARSAL MANAGEMENT

Another area where you will be well served by your organizational abilities is the planning and running of a rehearsal. Think about your 50-minute band rehearsal: As the bell rings, students are in their seats with their instruments ready to play. The order of warm-ups and music is on the board. The students have their music organized before the bell rings. Roll is taken in a non-invasive way, often by a student assistant with no rehearsal time wasted. Announcements are made. The band tunes quickly. Scales, arpeggios and a chorale are played. Immediately, this is followed by the first piece and so on. Final announcements are made and students are given a short amount of time to put their instruments away before the bell rings and they head to the next class. This routine is followed daily and consistently. This is not always the case in the average choral classroom.

Approach your choral rehearsals the same way you approached your band rehearsals: There should be no "down time" in the daily choral rehearsal. The rehearsals should always start on time. Don't say that it will start on time, do it! Music for the day should be on the board in order.

Students should have their choral folders and be seated before the bell rings (or the rehearsal period begins, if that isn't marked by a bell). Roll should be taken unobtrusively. Announcements should be brief. Effective and meaningful warm-ups should be quick and efficient. Pieces should be rehearsed in a logical and sequential order.

In some ways, rehearsal management is even more important in the choral classroom. Why? It is easier to have a disciplined band or orchestra classroom than it is to have a disciplined choral classroom. That's right, easier! It is a behavioral truth that when students are holding and/or playing an instrument either with their hands, embouchure or both, they are naturally less prone to discipline problems than choral students, who produce the music with the same part of the body that produces talking. I've always said that there are fewer discipline problems when a student has a horn in his mouth.

Teaching the voice requires greater classroom discipline than the teaching of an instrument.

Because of its personal nature, teaching the choral instrument (the voice) requires greater classroom discipline than the teaching of an external instrument does. Think about it. It takes a certain amount of time after the conductor has given a cutoff in a rehearsal for the horn to come off the lips and onto the lap. That is a grace period for the instrumental conductor. There is no grace period for the choral director.

When you stop or cut off a choir, you must have something important to say immediately or they will talk! If you cut off the ensemble and say something like, "Well, um, uh, when I was listening to that...uh...well...," you've lost them. If you cut off the group and stand there silently, you've lost them. Again, you must say something important and you must say it immediately. When you either wait too long to speak or say unimportant words, you actually train your students not to listen to you. In this situation, they are saying to themselves, "Why should I listen to the director? Nothing important is being said." If you do not know exactly what to say upon cutoff, keep conducting for a while until you know in your mind what to say, then cut off.

This is even truer when working with middle school students. Because of their transition from child to adulthood, this group of students becomes bored more easily and more quickly than other age groups. To maintain student interest in rehearsal, you must have a lower threshold for boredom than the students, and know that you have an even shorter grace period after cutoffs.

To maintain student interest in rehearsal, you must have a lower threshold for boredom than the students.

When conducting middle school choirs (or bands, as some of you may no doubt know), keep things moving, not dwelling on any one section or piece too long. There are times in any rehearsal when you must really dig into a particular section to polish it, but the master teacher knows when you're experiencing diminishing returns and need to move on. The purpose of rehearsal is to get a little better, not to achieve perfection.

When a class period is over, you and the students should be able to identify one or more specific behaviors that improved as a result of your instruction. If either of you cannot, then you didn't teach anything that day, regardless of the amount of time you and they spent in the classroom. Try this exercise with your students: At the conclusion of rehearsal, provide each student with a piece of note paper and have them write down one or more specific improvements that were made during that class period.

STUDENT LEADERSHIP

Another band-director tool I encourage you to draw on when it comes to classroom management is the instrumental approach to student leadership, which is a strong point in most bands and orchestras. In these ensembles, student leaders are often selected, not elected. Once a section leader is selected (I would suggest by the director), that student has a responsibility not only to be a leader in name, but in his or her modeling of the behavior, skills, and attitudes for the section. For example, if you are the trumpet section leader in the band, you are responsible for all of the elements that contribute to the quality of that section: organizing sectionals and proficiency checks on the music, checking that instruments are polished and music is organized, and, more importantly, displaying the skills and behaviors that *you* expect from the section.

All students want an organized, well-disciplined classroom (whether they admit it or not).

These kinds of student-leadership behaviors and practices can and should take place in your new choral classroom. The singers may be resistant at first, as this type of structure doesn't always exist in the "typical" choral classroom, but all music students want an organized, disciplined ensemble that is also of the highest musical standards. These practices will help them get there.

TEACHING CHORAL MUSIC

When you get right down to it, regardless of whether you're teaching band or choir or math or French, students are students. All students want an organized, well-disciplined classroom (whether they admit it or not). All students want a teacher who is fair. All students want a teacher who is caring. All students want a teacher who not only knows the subject matter, but also one who has a masterful delivery system. In other words, a teacher who knows the stuff and knows how to stuff it!

Regardless of instrumental or choral teaching, it is our job to lead the students to quality musical practice and performance. We must speak to them in language and terms that they understand. Take, for example, the concept of blend—if we make a lofty speech explaining blend in terms that require conceptual thinking beyond the students' experience, there will be little or no difference in their playing or singing.

All music students want a director who is musical. They want to get better musically and behaviorally every day and in every rehearsal. They want to hear you give them specific instructions. They want to know what they did incorrectly and more importantly how to correct it. They also want to know what they did well, and be praised for it.

Robinson's two Fs for successful teachers: "Be Friendly and Be Fair!" Come into every class, every day with a smile on your face and ready to make music!

Regardless of instrumental or choral teaching, it is our job to lead the students to quality musical practice and performance.

THE MUSIC MATTERS

As a band director, you have a lot going for you in the musical areas of choral directing as well. After many years of observing instrumental and choral directors, I've come to the opinion that instrumental conductors are much better (or perhaps, better-trained) technical conductors than choral directors. Let me explain. Instrumental conductors are trained with a baton and therefore, gestures are taught and usually executed in a very precise way. If one asks an instrumental conductor to conduct, with one hand, two measures of $\frac{4}{4}$ time with a cutoff/release on beat 4 of

A truly musical ensemble is created by a balance between the technical aspects and the musical and phrasing aspects.

the second measure, it is usually not a problem for this individual. If, however, one asks a choral conductor (who likely rarely uses a baton, or hasn't since Conducting 101) to do the exact same exercise, the urge to cutoff with the "other" hand often prohibits him or her from executing this task.

What does this mean for you, the band director teaching choirs? It means that you have yet another existing skill that will ease your transition into choral directing, particularly as you learn to pair it with the interpretive guidance that comes from the text we are fortunate to have in choral music.

CONDUCTING A CHOIR

A truly musical ensemble is created by a balance between the technical aspects (e.g., cues, releases, etc.) and the musical and phrasing aspects (e.g., dynamics, crescendos/decrescendos, etc.). This is true for both instrumental and choral ensembles. The role the conductor plays in achieving this balance is also the same for both.

We're all well aware of the conducting dos and don'ts, but even after 30 years, I still take time to remind myself that:

- All technical matters should be addressed with the primary hand (I prefer the right), and matters of expression and nuance should be relegated to the other hand (left). Mirror conducting produces a meaningless gesture with one of the hands.
- Every conducting gesture has a reciprocal effect on the sound we get from our ensemble whether it is a middle school choir or a college wind band. This realization *will* lead us to pay much more attention to our conducting gestures, and to make sure

that all show a high level of musicianship and sensitivity.

- Time spent practicing the conducting of a piece in front of a mirror is time well spent. You can see what you really look like and reinforce appropriate gestures that will be used for entrances, releases and dynamics, while maintaining eye contact.
- If we do not have a mental concept of what the piece is to sound like after it is rehearsed, it will be decided by the ensemble, and that can be very frightening!
- The purpose of the conductor is to bring attention to the ensemble. The more conservative and meaningful the conducting gestures are during a performance, the more the audience will be drawn to see and hear the students, rather than drawn to the exhibition that may be displayed on the podium.

BATON OR NO BATON

I find the use or non-use of the baton to be an interesting phenomenon. Not that many years ago, band or orchestra directors rarely would have been seen conducting without a baton. Now we see it quite often. Maestro Kurt Masur, former conductor of the New York Philharmonic, never uses a baton. Choral directors, on the other hand, have historically conducted without a baton.

I use a baton in the following three instances. Otherwise, I conduct choirs without a baton. I feel that I can get more nuances without a baton when conducting choral works.

1. When I am conducting a choir with orchestra.
2. When I am conducting a choral piece that was written originally for choir and orches-

Not that many years ago, band or orchestra directors rarely would have been seen conducting without a baton. Now we see it quite often.

Ultimately, if the conductor is a musician with effective teaching skills, he or she can be an excellent choral teacher and conductor.

tra and includes a highly realized piano reduction.

3. When I am conducting in the recording studio. (I find that studio singers, who are reading music on a raised music stand and singing and looking at me "through" a microphone, can better see the nuances out of their peripheral vision when they are given with a baton.)

Ultimately, if the conductor is a musician with effective teaching skills, he or she can be an excellent choral teacher and conductor both in rehearsals and performance (with or without a baton).

LET'S START AT THE VERY BEGINNING

A *DISCUSSION OF BREATHING, BLEND AND BALANCE, VOWEL PRODUCTION, AND PRACTICAL AND PURPOSEFUL CHORAL WARM-UP TECHNIQUES*

Just as your knowledge and experience as a band director have left you well prepared to address many of the extra-musical elements in the choral classroom, many of the fundamental components of creating a good choral sound can be taught by drawing on what you already know and do.

BREATHING AND POSTURE

Just as wind players must take a full, low breath to play their instrument, singers must take a full, low breath to activate their instrument. In my experience 90 percent of the problems in tone production—whether it's vocal tone production or tone production on any wind instrument—are due to improper breathing.

Ninety percent of the problems in tone production are due to improper breathing.

The same techniques you have employed to teach instrumentalists to take a full breath will be equally effective with singers. Whether "sipping air through a straw, then hissing the air out," or "dropping the air in with a surprise breath," use a technique that will allow a low breath, not a breath that raises the chest or shoulders.

And just as good posture is an important contributor to correct breathing for instrumentalists, it is important for singers to stand in a way that doesn't impede their breathing. While your singers obviously won't have to deal with holding a horn, they may be holding a choral folder, which will impact their posture.

In every festival I've judged and performance I've heard, I can predict the quality of the choir with almost absolute certainty before they even sing a note—I just look at the choir's posture. Similarly, just walking into a rehearsal room and observing the way a choir sits (or has been taught to sit) tells me a lot about how they are going to sing.

In rehearsals, students should:

1. Sit tall
2. Feet flat on the floor
3. Leaning slightly forward
4. Eyebrows up

In performance (or when standing in rehearsal) students should stand with:

1. Feet shoulder-width apart
2. Hands comfortably at the side, unless holding a music folder (students should hold folders with the left hand; the right is used to secure the folder and turn pages)

Just as good posture is an important contributor to correct breathing for instrumentalists, it is important for singers to stand in a way that doesn't impede their breathing.

3. Head straight up (or perpendicular to the floor, if they've had geometry!)
4. Eyebrows up

Keep instructions simple and be vigilant—good posture must be taught *and* reinforced to the students.

CHORAL WARM-UP TECHNIQUES

As a band director, what comprises your warm-up routine? It probably consists of:

1. Tuning
2. Scales and arpeggios
3. A chorale

What are the purposes of your warm-ups?

1. To get in tune, individually and collectively
2. To prepare students for technical passages
3. To achieve balance and blend

As a choral director, the warm-up routine will be somewhat different but the purposes are the same.

Like an instrumental warm-up, the choral warm-up should be quick and varied slightly in each rehearsal to avoid boredom. When the students enter the room, it is then they are the most ready for learning. Make the most of that time by not devoting too much of it to warming up. In a 50-minute or one-hour rehearsal, the warm-up should not exceed seven minutes. Why seven minutes? Because it allows for a little more than a minute for each of the five steps in the warm-up sequence presented below. Obviously in the first week of school, you'll want to spend more time warming up so that the students learn the routine, but once it's established, seven minutes should be plenty.

Like an instrumental warm-up, the choral warm-up should be quick and varied slightly in each rehearsal to avoid boredom.

Just as you'll likely find 10 variations in the warm-up routines of 10 band directors, there are many variations on the choral warm-up process. What follows is my standard warm-up routine, which consists of five sections and has worked very well for me. You may also want to use this routine to "re-warm-up" between pieces or at various times in the rehearsal.

CHORAL WARM-UP ROUTINE

1. Physical warm-up
2. Warming down
3. Warming up on all five vowels
4. Diction exercise
5. Chordal warm-up

PHYSICAL WARM-UP

Be creative with the physical warm-up and move quickly to the next step in the routine.

This can be virtually anything that is healthy and appropriate. For example:

- Stretch "to the sky" with the right hand, then the left hand.
- Head Down, Head Up, Head to the Right, Head to the Left. (Note that I avoid "rolling the head," as most orthopedic surgeons agree that this can cause neck and vertebrae damage.)

Some teachers will have students rub each others' necks or pat each other on the back, but I avoid this as it can be uncomfortable touching for students in junior high and high school.

Ultimately, when it comes to the physical warm-up, be creative, be aware of physical boundaries, and move quickly to the next step in the routine.

WARMING DOWN

To warm down, sing a descending five-note scale, from 5 to 1 or from *sol* to *do*, in a comfortable range on an "oo" vowel. Middle school/junior high choirs should begin in D major. High school choirs should begin in B-flat. Then, repeat this five-note scale up a half step. (See page 24 for several notated examples.)

Take care not to take this up in half steps too far, though, as you will warm "up" in the next exercise. Begin with just four or five half steps at the middle school/junior high school level and seven or eight half steps for high school singers.

A word here about the "oo" vowel: I always warm down on the "oo" vowel because it is the best naturally produced vowel. By starting here, students can be led to successful and beautiful vowel production sequentially, with the poorest produced vowels, the "ee" and the "eh," addressed once a well-produced vowel sound is established. The "oo" vowel also allows the "head" voice (sometimes called the top voice, or light side of the voice) to be brought down, rather than pushing the "chest" voice (sometimes called the "speaking" voice) up.

WARMING UP ON ALL VOWELS

To get the choir singing all five pure vowels ("ah," "eh," "ee," "oh," and "oo") have students sing an ascending and descending arpeggio on the 1-3-5-3-1 using the vowel sequence *noo, nee, noh, neh, naw.* Then repeat the pattern, ascending in half-steps. (See page 25.)

In order to give students the feeling of the top notes being easy and free to sing, you can instruct them to have their hands (or hand) start high on the 1 (*noo*) and come down as they sing the 5 (*noh*), then bring the hands back up for the final 1 (*naw*). This physical movement will help them sing freely and not reach for the high notes.

Physical movement will help students sing freely and not reach for the high notes.

(This kinesthetic technique is equally effective when rehearsing any ascending passage that needs to be sung more freely.)

Just as we warmed down on the "oo" vowel because it is the best naturally produced vowel, this warm-up exercise starts with the "oo." Doing so reinforces that vowels should be produced from an "oo" vowel perspective—so with the corners of the mouth in and vertical rather than horizontal. Further, the exterior of the mouth (aperture, in band terms) does not change as this warm-up is sung.

By keeping the shape of the exterior of the mouth the same, the "ee" vowel is formed with an "oo" on the lips and an "ee" inside the mouth. In the same way, the "eh" vowel has a shape of "oo," which gives it a sound I sometimes think of as "ehw." And the "ah" vowel is produced as "aw," like the words *law* or *saw*, rather than as "ah," which sometimes comes out like the childhood taunt *nah, nah, nah, nah-nah, nah* (not good for choral music).[1]

DICTION EXERCISE

As a choir director, one of your main musical responsibilities is making sure that the music's text is conveyed clearly to the listeners. Including a diction exercise in your warm-up will help singers improve their enunciation of consonants, which is necessary for text clarity.

Including a diction exercise in your warm-up will help singers improve their enunciation of consonants, which is necessary for text clarity.

---

[1] You've probably heard choirs warm-up all the vowels using the sequence *mah, meh, mee, moh, moo* or *mee, meh, mah, moh, moo*. (I used it myself for many years.) I've moved away from it because it teaches students to sing poorly produced vowels by starting from an "ah" vowel perspective, or even worse, an "ee" vowel perspective.

You can choose a particularly "wordy" section of a piece that you are going sing later in the rehearsal as your diction exercise, or you can use one of the exercises provide on page 26, moving it up or down in half steps as appropriate. Start slowly and increase the tempo as students are successful.

If sung correctly, with an enunciation that will carry to the audience, it will probably feel to the singers as if they are far overdoing their pronunciations. One of your challenges as a director is to help the students feel comfortable with this.

CHORDAL WARM-UP

The final step in an effective choral warm-up routine is a chordal warm-up in the key of the first piece you'll be rehearsing. Two voicings of an appropriate chordal warm-up for a middle school choir whose first piece is in the key of C are provided on page 27, as is a chordal warm-up for high school or adult choirs. Appendix A includes several collections of warm-up exercises to help you bring variety to this section of the warm-up routine.

BLEND AND BALANCE

Achieving blend and balance is one of the primary goals of any warm-up, and is central to quality music making. But what does "blend and balance" mean within a choral ensemble?

Balance is exactly the same in choral music as it is in instrumental music. Within a band, it means that within the trumpet section, or even the first trumpet section, there will be a balance in volume. In other words, no one individual player in the trumpet section is going to play louder than the next, whether the dynamic is

Balance is exactly the same in choral music as it is in instrumental music.

piano or *forte*. (Now there's a lifelong goal for every section, as students learn to be responsible for this aspect of musicianship in an ensemble setting.) The same is true for the clarinet section, trombone section, and all sections of the band. The same is also true for choirs—no one soprano should be louder than the other sopranos (another lifelong challenge!); no tenor should be louder than another tenor; no bass louder than another; and no alto louder than another.

There's also the matter of balance between sections. As you know, any instrumental ensemble should have a "pyramid" balance, so the lower the instrument plays, the more it should be heard. Why? Because of the physiology of the ear, higher pitches are perceived as louder than low pitches even if they are produced at the same volume. This means that if the piccolos play at the same volume as the tubas, the piccolos will be more prominent and dominate the sound.

You want a band or orchestra to be slightly bottom heavy; the same is true for choirs.

This same phenomenon applies to high and low voices, so the need for a pyramid balance between the sections of a choir is the same, too. The sopranos should be slightly softer than the altos, the altos should be slightly softer than the tenors, and the tenors should be slightly softer than the basses for a "perfect" balance. Said another way, you want a band or orchestra to be slightly bottom heavy; the same is true for choirs.

VOWEL PRODUCTION

Blend deals primarily with vowel production, specifically a consistent vertical vowel production. The concept of a vertical vowel was addressed earlier in this chapter as part of the "Warming Down" step (see page 16), but it merits further discussion because of its importance in creating a good choral sound.

The singer on the left is displaying a horizontal "ah" vowel while the singer on the right is achieving the desired vertical placement of the vowel.

Simply stated, consistent vertical vowel production means that all five of the pure vowels—"ah," "eh," "ee," "oh," and "oo"—are produced with a vertical, not horizontal, mouth.

To give an example of vertical vowels, let's look at the "ah" vowel. If you ask students to sing "ah," you will hear many, *many* variations of that vowel, most of which will be spread or horizontal, which equals bad choral production. If students are instead instructed to sing the "ah" vowel as "aw," as in *saw* or *law*, the vowel production and choral sound will improve dramatically. Why? Because producing the "ah" vowel as "aw" guarantees a vertical vowel—a vowel where the jaw is dropped and corners of the mouth are not spread.

Consistent vertical vowel production means that all five of the pure vowels are produced with a vertical, not horizontal, mouth.

Why does it need to be consistently sung as (and more importantly, consistently thought of as) "aw"? Because we must have *consistent* vertical vowel production to achieve choral blend. It only takes one person in the choir producing the "ah" vowel as "ah" instead of "aw" to destroy the blend. The students will hear the difference and so will you.[2]

DEALING WITH DIPHTHONGS

Focusing on the five pure vowels, and producing them in a consistent vertical way, also helps overcome that which strikes fear into the heart of many an untrained choral director—the diphthong. Diphthongs are simply syllables that contain more than one vowel sound, specifically the primary vowel and the vanishing vowel. Examples include the one-syllable words *I, my,* and *now.*

Although proper production of the diphthong is absolutely necessary to make beautiful choral music, it isn't the great mystery some make it out to be.

Although the proper production of the diphthong is absolutely necessary to make beautiful choral music, it isn't the great mystery some make it out to be. In fact, I tell my choirs that diphthongs do not exist. Say again?

Take the word *my.* When we break this diphthong into its two vowel sounds it becomes "mah-ee." If diphthongs do not exist, then *my* is simply pronounced "mah" or "maw." To put this in context, let's look at the familiar spiritual *My Lord, What a Morning.* Here, when the next word, *Lord,*

---

[2] I realize that my use of the "aw" vowel concept for "ah" and many of my thoughts regarding vowel production and warm-ups are simply that: my thoughts. Other choral pedagogues may have radically different ways of teaching vowel production and choral blend. The techniques presented here, however, have been proven to be effective in my teaching of untrained singers and resulted in student understanding and immediate success in achieving quality choral sound. Similarly, discussion of the International Phonetic Alphabet (IPA) has been omitted from this guide because it is seldom used at the middle and high school level.

is sung, the vanishing vowel in the diphthong *my,* which is "ee," will be heard, but only as a vanishing vowel eliding into *Lord.* Again, singers will easily understand the simplicity of this concept and your choral music will sound beautiful, incorporating the purity of the primary vowel in words that contain diphthongs.

TUNING

I remember when I was teaching band: each student was to go individually to the stroboscope and tune prior to the band rehearsal. Then we quickly did harmonic and melodic tuning in the rehearsal. But how do you "tune" the choir? While you can't "push in" or "pull out" a voice, teaching proper breath support through effective warm-ups will give students a much better chance of singing a note in tune.

It's also important to remember that "You can't tune wrong notes!" applies to singers too. We've all seen it: a new teacher telling the band to play in tune but failing to notice that someone in the trumpet section is pushing down the wrong valve. If a singer is out of the bandwidth of a correct note, it is simply a wrong note, not out of tune.

✳   ✳   ✳

A thoughtful and sequential warm-up is the key to achieving a quality choral sound. Band directors know this. Every quality band rehearsal begins with a quality and effective warm-up. The same is true for choir. Once band directors learn how to teach wonderful vowels and diction, they will be well on their way to producing beautiful choral singing!

While you can't "push in" or "pull out" a voice, teaching proper breath support through effective warm-ups will give students a much better chance of singing a note in tune.

WARMING DOWN

MIDDLE SCHOOL/JUNIOR HIGH

Noo Noo Noo Noo Noo

HIGH SCHOOL

Noo Noo Noo Noo Noo

WARMING UP ON ALL VOWELS

Diction Exercises

Ev - 'ry note we sing must be with dic - tion un - der - stood!

Ev - 'ry note we sing must be with dic - tion un - der - stood!

Ma - ma made me mash my M and Ms.

Ches - ter Chee - tah chewed a chunk of cheap ched - dar cheese. __

CHORDAL WARM-UPS

MIDDLE SCHOOL

MIDDLE SCHOOL (ALTERNATE VOICING)

HIGH SCHOOL

GOOD TO GREAT

UNDERSTANDING TEXT AND PHRASING—THE DIFFERENCE BETWEEN GOOD CHOIRS AND GREAT CHOIRS

One realization I came to quickly when I began conducting choirs is that the text is the greatest tool at a choir director's disposal. Vowels, intonation, precise entrances, and releases are extremely important, but they are simply a vehicle for the text, and it is the text that guides those musical decisions.

TEXT ACCENTS

Every sentence that we speak makes sense because of the rise and fall of the pitch and inflection, and the accents that we place on the important words and syllables. The same is true when we sing. I have often said to choirs, "The difference between good choirs and great choirs is text accents!"

The difference between good choirs and great choirs is text accents.

Here is an example of the power of text accents using a lyric from *The River Sleeps Beneath the Sky,* with text by Paul Laurence Dunbar and music by Mary Lynn Lightfoot.[1]

> *The river sleeps beneath the sky and holds the shadows to its breast.*

Say this lyric dramatically. When you do, you'll probably speak it as shown below, with the accented syllables indicated in bold, and will note that the important words are *river, sky, shadows,* and *breast.*

> *The **river** sleeps be**neath** the sky and holds the **shad**ows to its breast.*

Now, look at this lyric in its musical context:

Sing the phrase with no accents. Sing it again, accenting the words with more than one syllable (*river, beneath, shadows*) as you spoke them in the previous exercise. Now, sing it while accenting the appropriate syllables *and* the other important words (*sky* and *breast*) while deemphasizing the less-important words (*the, and, to, its*). Notice how the music comes to life!

---

[1] *The River Sleeps Beneath the Sky* is published by Heritage Music Press in four voicings: SATB (product number 15/1506H); SSA (15/1306H); Three-part Mixed (15/1305H); and Two-part (15/1304H).

TREATMENT OF LONG NOTES

Text accents are an essential component of phrasing. Certainly, when breaths are taken is another, as is the treatment of long notes. I tell choirs, "All long notes crescendo to the next note or rest unless the director tells you something different. Why? That's what musicians do!"

Let's revisit the phrase on the previous page and consider how the long notes should be treated.

Where are the long notes in these four measures? *Sleeps, sky*, and *breast*. These words should have a slight crescendo to them. Add this element to the text accents established previously and you have taken the music from notes, rests, rhythms, appropriate vowels, and intonation to true music-making!

MORE THAN ONE NOTE WITHIN A SYLLABLE

Not unlike slurred notes in instrumental music, choral music often includes repeated or multiple notes within a syllable. How these notes are treated will further determine the beauty and meaning of the music.

A general rule for phrasing in this circumstance is, where there is more than one note in a given syllable, all notes after the first note will be softer. There may be exceptions to this, such as when an explicit crescendo is written for the series of notes in the *melisma*,[2] but this approach will give students a starting point for how to treat these notes musically in the context of a phrase.

Choral music often includes repeated or multiple notes within a syllable. How these notes are treated will further determine the beauty and meaning of the music.

---

2 *Melisma* is a group of notes sung to a single syllable.

Let's look at an example from *Sanctus*, by Victor C. Johnson.[3]

What are the syllables with more than one note? *Sanc* and *tus* in the first measure, *Sanc* in the second, and *De* and *us* in the fourth. The first element of phrasing to be addressed is text accents. Based on what we discussed previously, this phrase would be accented as:

Sanc*tus*, Sanc*tus*, Do*mi*nus De*us*

Most untrained singers think, "if the note goes up, it must be louder."

Now to factor in where multiple notes are sung on one syllable. On *Sanc* in the first measure notice how the second note goes up. Most untrained singers (and untrained choral directors) think, "if the note goes up, it must be louder," and we often hear that erroneous interpretation in performance. Based on our established rule that any note after the first should be softer, the singers must consciously and audibly decrescendo on the second note.

Another element of phrasing that must be taken into account in this example is the treatment of long notes. In measure 2, the second syllable of *Sanctus* should be unaccented (because of the text accent), but would crescendo at the end

---

[3] *Sanctus (Quoting Pachelbel's "Canon in D")* is published by Heritage Music Press in two voicings: SATB (15/2255H) and SAB (15/2241H).

because it is a long note (because "all long notes crescendo to the next note or rest").

It should also be noted that, in this example, the technique of crescendoing on long notes will also assist in producing a four-measure phrase. I rarely say anything in rehearsals about not breathing between notes; I simply have the choir crescendo. You cannot crescendo and breathe at the same time!

You cannot crescendo and breathe at the same time!

PUTTING IT ALL TOGETHER

If one were to over-edit this example and notate all three main phrasing considerations—text accents, the treatment of long notes, and phrasing when there is more than one note within a syllable—it would look like this:

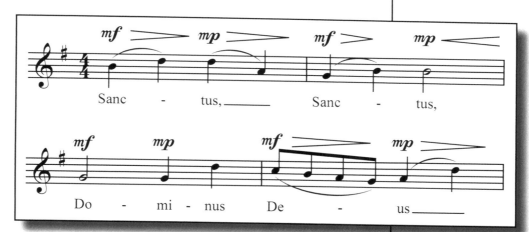

Of course, one would not mark the score in this way, but it does show how the text is the guide to all phrasing.[4] Given precise intonation and beautiful uniform vowels, the added elements of text accents and phrasing will be the icing on the cake of beautiful choral music that realizes the ultimate goal of choral music—to tell a story through song.

---

[4] The decrescendo on beats 3 and 4 in the fourth measure of this example is included to illustrate the concepts being discussed here. In the arrangement, there is a *forte* dynamic in measure 5, which Mr. Johnson prepares with a crescendo on beats 3 and 4 of measure 4.

MY SOP FOR THE SAB IS MIA

AN OVERVIEW OF CHORAL ENSEMBLES AND A GUIDE TO SELECTING APPROPRIATE LITERATURE FOR EACH

We all have our standard operating procedure for choosing what our bands will play this year. But how do we pick music for our choirs, and what do all those letters in their names mean? Read on for descriptions of the most common choral ensembles and guidelines for selecting music that is appropriate for each.

TYPES OF CHORAL ENSEMBLES

TREBLE CHOIRS

Treble choirs are generally found in elementary and middle school/junior high settings and will include females and males with unchanged voices. These choirs will sing primarily in unison and two parts. Music for these choirs will be designated as SA (meaning Soprano and Alto)

Be aware that some pieces for treble choirs are simply a two-part arrangement of an SATB piece. If not written carefully, this can result in an arrangement with parts that are extremely difficult in range and intervals.

or Two-part (meaning Part I is the top part and Part II is the lower part).

One must be very selective when choosing music for this type of choir. Rounds and canons work well for treble choirs, and there are many fine arrangements of classics by Mozart, Vivaldi and other masters for these voices. Be aware that some pieces are simply a two-part arrangement of an SATB piece. If not written carefully, this can result in an arrangement with parts that are extremely difficult in range and intervals. Further, the text may or may not be appropriate for elementary students (as the piece was originally written for older performers).

When evaluating music for treble choirs, pay particular attention to the ranges. A good rule of thumb is to make sure the range is contained "in the staff," so nothing higher than G on top of the staff and nothing lower than B below middle C.

CHANGED BOYS' VOICES

If some of the boys in your treble choir have changed voices, you may use two-part arrangements by dividing the girls and unchanged boys between Parts I and II (or S and A). Then, have the changed boys double Part I (or the soprano part) down an octave. Part II (or the alto part) should rarely be doubled down the octave. This is a wonderful way to introduce singing to boys with changed voices.

SSA CHOIRS

Whereas treble choirs tend to be elementary and middle school/junior high choirs, SSA (Soprano I, Soprano II, Alto) choirs are common in high school and college and university settings. The age difference, and the fact that SSA choirs sing in three parts, are the main differences between the two.

There is a wealth of beautiful repertoire in all styles for SSA choirs, from Broadway and popular music to folk songs to classics and originals. Again, consider text, ranges and appropriate level of difficulty for the choir.

Consider text, ranges and appropriate level of difficulty for the choir.

MEN'S CHOIRS

Another common ensemble at the high school and college level is the men's choir. Typically voicings for this group include TB, TTB or TTBB. Like women's choirs, repertoire is available in all styles and should be evaluated based on text, ranges and difficulty.

SAB AND THREE-PART MIXED CHOIRS

Typically found at the middle school/junior high level, three-part mixed choirs are made up of girls and boys with both changed and unchanged voices, with the girls and unchanged boys singing Parts I and II and the boys with changed voices singing Part III. SAB choirs include girls and boys, most of whose voices have changed. While they are found at the junior high/middle school levels, they may be very appropriate for beginning (ninth/tenth grade) high school choirs.

What is the difference between SAB and Three-part Mixed literature?[1] Three-part Mixed music is, for the most part, limited in Part III to a six-note range of F below middle C to D above. In SAB, the baritone part can have a range of "anything and anywhere." You must be very cautious when selecting SAB for the changed boys' voices in your choir. Some baritone parts may be in the bass range, some in the tenor range, and some in both! Generally, publishers and writers try to keep the baritone range from around a B-flat an

---

[1] This is actually a test question for my college students. Why? Because so many people, including veteran choral teachers, don't know!

octave below middle C to middle C or D above middle C, but that is far from a steadfast rule.

The amount of three-part mixed and SAB literature has increased dramatically over the past 15 years. There is appropriate and quality literature for these voices in all styles, including classics, folk song arrangements, originals, and popular music. Again, consider the ranges, text and appropriate difficulty for your group.

SATB Concert Choirs

Concert choirs are generally of sufficient size and variety of voices to justify SATB (Soprano, Alto, Tenor, Bass) literature, both accompanied and *a cappella*.

Balance may be a problem, but I caution you to use the voices in their appropriate natural range. In other words, better to have six sopranos, nine altos, three tenors, and five basses then to force the voices into unhealthy ranges.

The number of singers in this type of group will vary, as will the number of singers on each part. You may walk into a program in its first year or two where there are only 23 singers, 15 females and eight males. Balance may be a problem, but I caution you to use the voices in their appropriate natural range. In other words, better to have six sopranos, nine altos, three tenors, and five basses then to force the voices into unhealthy ranges. (Remember, as discussed in Chapter 2, balance is not determined by the number of singers in each section.)

SATB is the most common voicing for choirs; therefore you will find the greatest selection of literature in this voicing. I would encourage you to have a variety of repertoire for your singers, from arrangements of folk songs to classical repertoire, from Mozart to Vivaldi. Spirituals can be very well done in SATB literature. In addition, original contemporary works may be appropriate; however, be careful with esoteric pieces that may require more work for beginning choirs than the time to teach them is worth.

SHOW AND JAZZ CHOIRS

Show choirs have appeared in school curricula since the early 1970s, performing mainly arrangements of popular and Broadway show tunes. These ensembles are often accompanied by at least piano, bass guitar, drums, and even a horn section with two trumpets, tenor saxophone and trombone.

The performances of these groups tend to be short and in the context of festivals or competitions, so feature only an opening number, a show tune, a ballad, and a high-energy closing piece. The perception of show choirs has been controversial because many of these popular groups put such emphasis on the dance, movements, outfits, and other visual accessories that the quality of the choral singing and the singers' vocal health suffers. Remember that movement or choreography, if used, should always support and enhance the music, not detract from it.

Jazz choirs sing jazz standards and original repertoire in a jazz style but without choreography. Many times jazz choral arrangements extend beyond the four parts of SATB, often utilizing six, eight or more parts to accommodate the jazz chords and voicings.

A very nice "show" program shared by both ensembles could be: opening number (choreographed), Broadway tune (choreographed), *a cappella* jazz ballad (non-choreographed), up-tempo swing (non-choreographed), and a closing up-tempo piece (choreographed).

Many times jazz choral arrangements extend beyond the four parts of SATB, often utilizing six, eight or more parts to accommodate the jazz chords and voicings.

MADRIGAL GROUPS

Madrigal groups are quite popular at the high school level. As the name would suggest, they perform primarily *a cappella* Renaissance secular music. Much of the music is SATB, although there are many SAB and Three-part Mixed arrangements of madrigals. Often, the same group of singers will be both the madrigal group and the show choir, depending on the time of year or concert needs.

AGE AND EXPERIENCE OF THE SINGERS

These are two separate considerations, with age sometimes being an immediate disqualifier of some literature.

AGE

The consideration of age is really about the maturation of the voices—both because of the amount of training they've had and the physical development of the instrument. Good voice teachers know that high school singers should not sing most opera arias, as they are written for mature voices. The same is true for choral music. Singing in the extremes of register, be it high or low, and volume, particularly a loud volume, is not healthy or appropriate for undeveloped young voices. This is true for middle school and high school voices.

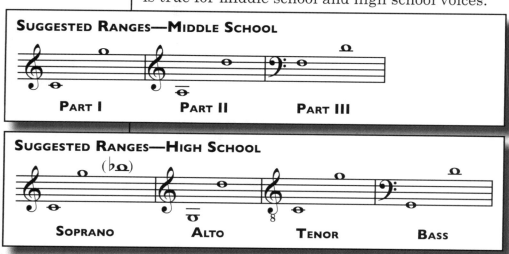

SUGGESTED RANGES—MIDDLE SCHOOL

PART I   PART II   PART III

SUGGESTED RANGES—HIGH SCHOOL

SOPRANO   ALTO   TENOR   BASS

Many high school directors try to do high-level college and professional repertoire with their singers, yet the voices are not sufficiently developed to sing healthily with precision. I hear many high school choirs try to perform authentic spirituals in eight or more parts with 16- and 17-year-old students. It is the truly exceptional choir (not to mention the true exception among choirs) that is prepared developmentally and musically to perform this repertoire.

EXPERIENCE

Unlike age, experience is multifaceted and hinges on the following:

1. **The maturity of the program.** Has the program had a different director every year or two? Or, has the director been there for 10 years?
2. **The experience of the individual singers in the choir.** Is this the first year in choir for over half of the students? Or, have two-thirds of the seniors (or 8th graders, if a middle school choir) been in the program for the past three or four years?

I often tell my college music education students that it takes about five years to learn how to teach because only then do you see the results of your teaching on the same students as they proceed through the program. If a majority of your students are leaving the program every year, you need to look at what you're doing that could be causing attrition. If you select and perform quality music that is appropriate for the ensemble and have solid rehearsal techniques, students will find the choir stimulating, challenging and fun. If one or both of those ingredients is missing, attrition will naturally increase.

If you select and perform quality music that is appropriate for the ensemble and have solid rehearsal techniques, students will find the choir stimulating, challenging and fun. If one or both of those ingredients is missing, attrition will naturally increase.

TYPE OF PROGRAM OR CONCERT

Programming and music selection is contextual; that is, you must learn to choose the appropriate music for the appropriate program.

EVALUATIVE FESTIVAL PROGRAMS

Evaluation festivals often have a limited time frame. For example, 20 or 30 minutes are allotted to assemble on stage, perform, and exit the stage. If one is participating in a concert choir festival category, regardless of age group, the director must avoid selecting non-concert choir music. In other words, show tunes, jazz and popular music should be avoided. Instead, if performing three pieces, consider selecting:

If one is participating in a concert choir festival category, regardless of age group, the director must avoid selecting non-concert choir music.

1. A classical piece at a moderate to fast tempo[2]
2. A slower piece in a different style
3. An up-tempo folk song, contemporary concert piece, or spiritual

If entering a festival in a show choir or jazz choir category, you'll obviously want to choose music that is appropriate for that category.

HOLIDAY CONCERTS

This is an area of programming that has probably seen the most change in the past 20 years. Many school districts will not allow any religious music to be performed. Given the fact that most of the winter holidays, from Christmas to Hanukkah, are religious celebrations, it is difficult to perform holiday music that is not from the church, regardless of language.

---

[2] In this instance, and in choral music in general, classical refers to all Western art music, not just the music of the Classical period.

Take, for example, Palestrina's *Adoramus Te, Christe.* It has become a standard concert choir piece but, because of its text, it may not be performed in some school districts. If your decision to program it, or other music with a sacred text, is questioned by parents or administrators, remind them that it is being sung to expand students' musical knowledge and not to promote any religious doctrine.[3] (On the other hand, choosing a piece from the genre of contemporary Christian music is likely not appropriate in most school settings.)

Your holiday programming should include music of many cultures as well as the many secular holiday pieces that are available. If possible, make the holiday concert a joint performance with the band, and perform a combined number or two. Also, incorporate small choral groups (madrigals, trios, quartets) and soloists. Audiences want variety, not just ten pieces in a row by the choir. Be creative and make your holiday concerts exciting.

Your holiday programming should include music of many cultures as well as the many secular holiday pieces that are available.

Spring Concerts

Spring concerts can incorporate many of the festival pieces that you have prepared. Other things to think about when selecting repertoire for your spring concert:

- Include lighter pieces
- Have both the full choir and smaller ensembles perform
- Feature soloists with the choir, as well as instrumentalists (many pieces of choral music have a flute accompaniment)
- Include music of other cultures (there is a rich tradition of African, Hispanic and

---

[3] For more information on performing music with a sacred text, visit the "Information on Music Education" portion of MENC's Web site (www.menc.org) and follow the "Sacred Music" link.

Hebrew choral music) and music in other languages (Latin, French, Spanish and German are all very singable and most quality arrangements will include a pronunciation guide)

The spring concert is also a time to perform a piece that acknowledges those in your choir who are graduating.

✳ ✳ ✳

There is no greater challenge than selecting choral music which is appropriate for the age and experience of the choir.

There is no greater challenge than selecting choral music which is appropriate for the age and experience of the choir, as well as appropriate for the different types of choirs and the variety of concert formats. By paying careful attention to all three of these considerations, though, your rehearsals and performances and the attitude of your students will culminate in a positive choral learning experience for all.

AFTERWORD:
AND IN THE END

DISCOVERING THE JOYS
OF TEACHING CHORAL MUSIC

As a former band director who has now been in love with teaching choral music for many years, I realize more and more that when we are teaching the human instrument—the voice—as opposed to "external" instruments, there are so many areas and specifics that we no longer have to worry about:

When we are teaching voice, there are many things we no longer have to worry about.

- Valve oil
- Stuck mouthpieces
- Dry woodwind pads
- Rosin
- Lost 3rd Trumpet music
- Broken reeds
- Lyres
- Switching a student's instrument from clarinet to bassoon (or clarinet to trombone!)
- Marching band practice
- Friday night football game marching shows

The complete list, as you well know, could fill volumes. I have the greatest respect for band and orchestra directors, as they have some of the toughest teaching jobs on the planet. Fortunately, the challenges that we encountered as band directors enable us to look at the added opportunities that we have as choral directors.

For band and orchestra directors who are always working with external instruments, the preparation required to be able to get to the actual music-making can be significant. What a joy to be able to take those same energies and use that precious time to work on the music in both breadth and depth. In choral music, we basically sit or stand with good posture, breathe and—given quality choral music and instruction—begin to sing and make music immediately with no mechanical impediments.

Give us bright, shining faces and we can jump into the art and skill of choral singing immediately. This does not discount the fact that the teaching and making of quality choral music and mature choral musicians is a lifelong pursuit.

Never forget that in choral music we have the distinct advantage of telling a story through song, regardless of language.

I hope that your reading of this book has shown you that you already possess many of the musical skills needed to teach choral music, given the additional knowledge and awareness of two key areas: the voice (particularly vowel production) and repertoire selection. I cannot emphasize enough how beneficial to music-making the presence of text is. Never forget that in choral music we have the distinct advantage of telling a story through song, regardless of language.

As a choral director, instead of applying those organizational skills you already possess to managing the items listed on the previous page (value oil, mouthpieces, reeds...), you can spend your time with activities more closely connected to building musicianship:

- **Rehearsal planning.** Start from the time they walk into the room. Establish a smooth process for getting music to students and taking attendance. Address seated and standing posture, warm-ups, and the sequence of pieces to be rehearsed.
- **Thoughtful literature selection.** Make the most of every precious dollar that you have to spend on music by attending workshops, reading sessions and conventions, and accessing the many Web sites that allow you to see and hear the music before you purchase it, matching the music with each ensemble's level of experience.
- **Rewarding performances**. Craft programs that are a joy for both the students and audience, with a variety of styles and ensembles, but always with the highest quality of musicianship.

Whether by your own decision or the decision of others, you have been given the opportunity to teach choral music. What great joy and fulfillment there is for the teacher, students and audience when rehearsing and performing choral music at the highest level!

As a choral director, you can spend your time with activities more closely connected to building musicianship.

A | RESOURCES FOR THE CHORAL DIRECTOR

WARM-UP EXERCISES AND VOCALISES

Building Beautiful Voices
A concise yet comprehensive study of vocal technique for the choral rehearsal or private instruction
By Paul Nesheim with Weston Noble
Roger Dean Publishing Co. (ISBN: 0-89328-138-7)

The Choral Warm-Up Collection
A Sourcebook of 167 Choral Warm-Ups Contributed by 51 Choral Directors
Ed. Sally K. Albrecht
Alfred Publishing (ISBN: 0-73903-052-3)

The Complete Choral Warm-up Book
By Jay Althouse and Russell L. Robinson
Alfred Publishing (ISBN: 0-88284-657-4)

Warm-Ups by the Dozen, Set 1
By Russell L. Robinson
Alfred Publishing
UPC: 654979993384 (SATB)
UPC: 654979993391 (SAB/3-Part Mixed)
UPC: 654979993407 (2-Part)

49

Warm-Ups by the Dozen, Set 2
By Russell L. Robinson
Alfred Publishing
UPC: 654979063803 (SATB)
UPC: 654979063810 (3-Part Mixed)
UPC: 654979063827 (2-Part)

Texts on the Choral Art

The Choral Director's Guide to Sanity...and Success!
How to Develop a Flourishing Middle School/Junior High School Choral Program
By Randy Pagel with Linda Spevacek
Heritage Music Press (ISBN: 0-89328-172-7)

The Complete Guide to Teaching Vocal Jazz
By Steve Zegree
Heritage Music Press (ISBN: 0-89328-153-0)

From the Trenches
Real Insights from Real Choral Educators
By Catherine Pfeiler-Bielawski and Nancy Jorgensen
Heritage Music Press (ISBN: 0-89328-159-X)

In Search of Musical Excellence
Taking Advantage of Varied Learning Styles
By Sally Herman
Roger Dean Publishing Co. (ISBN: 0-89328-118-2)

Precision Conducting: Achieving Choral Blend and Balance
By Timothy W. Sharp
Roger Dean Publishing Co. (ISBN: 0-89328-043-7)

Sharing Secrets
A Step-by-Step Journey from Unison to Two-Part Singing
By Phyllis Wolfe White and Karen Bodoin
Heritage Music Press (ISBN: 0-89328-160-3)

Way Over in Beulah Lan'
Understanding and Performing the Negro Spiritual
By Dr. André J. Thomas
Heritage Music Press (ISBN: 0-89328-723-7)

OTHER RESOURCES OF INTEREST

Hogey's Journey
A Memoir
By Eph Ehly
Heritage Music Press (ISBN: 0-89328-220-0)

Translations and Annotations of Choral Repertoire
Volume I: Sacred Latin Texts
Compiled and annotated by Ron Jeffers
earthsongs (ISBN: 0-9621532-1-4)

INSTRUCTIONAL DVDs

Body, Mind, Spirit, Voice
*A documentary from the 14th-annual National Choral Conference
    with Dr. Anton Armstrong and Dr. André J. Thomas, featuring
    The American Boy Choir*
The American Boychoir School, distributed by
The Lorenz Corporation (UPC: 000308108712)

The Choral Director as Voice Teacher
By Linda Spevacek
Heritage Music Press (UPC: 000308109559)

Creative Rehearsal Techniques for Today's Choral Classroom
Maintaining Student Interest and Maximizing Their Musicianship
By Russell L. Robinson
Alfred Publishing (UPC: 038081261836)

Jazz Style and Improvisation for Choirs
By Russell L. Robinson
Alfred Publishing (UPC: 654979099642)

Middle School Singers
Turning Their Energy into Wonderful Choirs
By Russell L. Robinson
Alfred Publishing (UPC: 038081297255)

APPENDIX B | PUBLISHERS OF EDUCATIONAL CHORAL MUSIC

Alfred Publishing Company
P.O. Box 10003
Van Nuys, CA 91410-0003
Phone: (818) 892-2452
Fax: (818) 830-6252
customerservice@alfred.com
www.alfred.com

Alliance Publications, Inc.
P.O. Box 131977
Houston, TX 77219-1977
Phone: (713) 868-9980
Fax: (713) 802-2988
info@alliancemusic.com
www.alliancemusic.com

Boosey & Hawkes, Inc.
35 East 21st Street
New York, NY 10010-6212
Phone: (212) 358-5300
Fax: (212) 358-5305
info.ny@boosey.com
www.boosey.com

BriLee Music Publishing Co.
Distributed by Carl Fischer, LLC
65 Bleecker Street
New York, NY 10012
Phone: (212) 777-0900
Fax: (212) 477-6996
cf-info@carlfischer.com
www.carlfischer.com

Carl Fischer, LLC
65 Bleecker Street
New York, NY 10012
Phone: (212) 777-0900
Fax: (212) 477-6996
cf-info@carlfischer.com
www.carlfischer.com

Colla Voce Music, Inc.
4600 Sunset Avenue, #83
Indianapolis, IN 46208
Phone: (317) 466-0624
Fax: (317) 466-0638
info@collavoce.com
www.collavoce.com

Hal Leonard Corporation
P.O. Box 13819
Milwaukee, WI 53213
Phone: (414) 774-3630
Fax: (414) 774-3259
www.halleonard.com

Heritage Music Press
A Lorenz Company
P.O. Box 802
Dayton, OH 45401-0802
Phone: (937) 228-6118
Fax: (937) 223-2042
info@lorenz.com
www.lorenz.com

Hinshaw Music, Inc.
P.O. Box 470
Chapel Hill, NC 27514
Phone: (919) 933-1691
Fax: (919) 967-3399
www.hinshawmusic.com

Mark Foster Music Co.
A division of Shawnee Press, Inc.
1107 17th Avenue South
Nashville, TN 37212
Phone: (800) 962-8584
Fax: (615) 320-7306
info@shawneepress.com
www.shawneepress.com

Roger Dean Publishing Co.
A Lorenz Company
P.O. Box 802
Dayton, OH 45401-0802
Phone: (937) 228-6118
Fax: (937) 223-2042
info@lorenz.com
www.lorenz.com

Shawnee Press, Inc.
1107 17th Avenue South
Nashville, TN 37212
Phone: (800) 962-8584
Fax: (615) 320-7306
info@shawneepress.com
www.shawneepress.com

Walton Music
Distributed by Hal Leonard Corporation
P.O. Box 13819
Milwaukee, WI 53213
Phone: (414) 774-3630
Fax: (414) 774-3259
www.halleonard.com

ABOUT THE AUTHOR

Dr. Russell L. Robinson has been on the faculty at the University
of Florida since 1984, where he is Professor of Music, Area Head
of Music Education and Education Liaison for the College of Fine
Arts, and has been the recipient of numerous teaching awards and
honors. Highly in demand, Dr. Robinson has made over 300 appear-
ances as a conductor and presenter at festivals, workshops, honor
choirs, all-state choirs, and state, regional, national and international conferences in North America, Europe, China, Singapore,
Central and South America, Thailand, Japan, Africa, and Australia.
As a conductor, he has appeared at Carnegie Hall, the Kennedy
Center, Boston's Symphony Hall, the White House, the Wiesbaden
Opera House, the Linz (Austria) Festival, and Washington's National Cathedral. He is a past President of the Florida Music Educa-

tors Association, Interim Associate Dean of the UF College of Fine Arts, National Collegiate Chair for the Music Educators National Conference (MENC), and is the current MENC Choral Adviser in the national publication *Teaching Music*. Dr. Robinson is a published author, composer and arranger with over 200 publications in print, including choral compositions, arrangements, articles, books, instructional videos, and DVDs. For more information about these publications, as well as his extensive workshop schedule, visit www. russellrobinson.com.